SMART MONEY:

How to Manage Your Finance Wisely

BY

AVIN ALEXANDER INKWELL

SMART MONEY: How To Manage Your Finance Wisely

PREFACE

Managing your finances is one of the most crucial skills you can acquire in life. As the renowned businessman Warren Buffett said, "Someone is sitting in the shade today because someone planted a tree a long time ago." The earlier you begin managing your finances wisely, the more likely you are to enjoy a comfortable future.

Smart Money is a practical guide that aims to help you take control of your financial future. Whether you're striving to fulfill a cherished dream or plan for the future, being smart with your money can assist you in achieving your objectives and living the life you desire. This comprehensive guide covers a wide range of topics, including budgeting, debt management, investing, wealth creation, and cultivating a positive money mindset.

The book is composed in a simple, yet engaging style, rendering it accessible to readers of all ages and financial backgrounds. Whether you're starting out on your career path or are a seasoned professional, Smart Money provides valuable insights and practical advice to help you achieve your financial goals.

Smart Money is not just another personal finance book. It is a comprehensive guide that takes readers on a journey to financial freedom. The book is packed with valuable information, tips, and strategies that readers can apply to their own lives.

The author understands that managing finances can be daunting, so they have written the book in a simple and engaging style, making it accessible to readers of all financial backgrounds. The book is structured in a way that allows readers to easily navigate the topics that interest them most.

Throughout the book, the author emphasizes the importance of cultivating a positive money mindset. They show readers how to overcome common money mindset obstacles and provide practical tips to help them develop a healthy relationship with money.

Smart Money also provides readers with a wealth of resources to help them on their financial journey. It includes recommendations for further reading, websites, and tools to help readers take control of their finances.

As Benjamin Franklin once famously said, "An investment in knowledge pays the best interest." With Smart Money, you'll have access to a wealth of knowledge and resources that will aid you in building a strong financial foundation.

In short, Smart Money is not just a book, it's a practical guide that will assist you in taking the reins of your financial future and lead you to a life of financial stability, security, and success.

CONTENTS

INTRODUCTION

In a bustling city, there lived six individuals who were struggling with their finances. Maya, John, Ava, Alex, Carlos, and Sarah were all leading different lives, but they shared a common struggle - managing their money.

Maya was a college student who was eager to learn about money and its nuances. John was a middle-aged father of two struggling to make ends meet. Alex was a recent college graduate who landed his first job. Ava a recent divorcee who is struggling with her finances and how she become debt free. Carlos was a retiree who wants to grow his wealth but is hesitant to start investing. Sarah a successful business owner looking to become financially independent.

Despite their differences, these six individuals crossed paths and realized that they could help each other overcome their financial challenges. They decided to form a support group, where they could share their experiences, learn from each other, and support each other through their financial journeys.

As they embarked on their journey together, Maya learned about the basics of money and how it worked. John created a budget, tracked his income and expenses, and set financial goals. Alex learned how to save more money. Ava managed to pay off her debts and started building her credit score. Carlos diversified his investment portfolio and explored new opportunities. And Sarah helped them all cultivate a positive money mindset while achieving financial independence.

Together, they learned the importance of financial education, budgeting, debt management, investing, building passive income streams, and achieving financial independence. They faced challenges, setbacks, and obstacles, but they persevered and supported each other through thick and thin.

They had become a family of sorts, united by their common struggle and their determination to achieve financial freedom.

SMART MONEY: How To Manage Your Finance Wisely

CHAPTER 1: UNDERSTANDING MONEY

Maya was a bright and ambitious college student, eager to learn about the world around her. She had always been interested in economics and finance, but the more she learned, the more confused she became.

One day, Maya was talking to her father about money and investments, and she realized she didn't fully understand how they worked. She knew the basics, but there were so many different terms and concepts that she couldn't quite grasp. Her father tried to explain things to her, but Maya felt overwhelmed and frustrated.

Determined to understand money, Maya started doing her own research. She read books, articles, and watched videos online. She talked to financial advisors and attended workshops. The more she learned, the more she realized how important it was to have a solid understanding of money and how it works.

Eventually, Maya's hard work paid off. She began to understand the nuances of investing, saving, and budgeting. She felt empowered and confident in her ability to make smart financial decisions. Maya even started sharing what she learned with her friends and family, hoping to help others avoid the confusion she had experienced.

Through her journey, Maya realized that understanding money is a vital life skill that everyone should have. She was grateful for the opportunity to learn and grow, and she hoped to inspire others to do the same.

WHAT IS MONEY AND HOW IT WORKS

Money is a concept that has fascinated humans for centuries. From the early days of bartering to the introduction of coins and paper money, money has played a vital role in shaping human society. It is a medium of exchange that allows us to buy goods and services, a unit of account that helps us measure the value of things, and a store of value that allows us to save our wealth for future use.

Maya, a young college student, was eager to learn more about money and its nuances. She knew that understanding money was the key to managing her finances wisely and achieving financial success. As she delved deeper into the subject, Maya learned that money has evolved over time to adapt to the changing needs of society.

She learned about the different types of money, such as fiat money, commodity money, and digital money, and was amazed by how money had adapted to the changing times. Maya also learned that having a positive money mindset was essential for financial success. She realized that taking control of her finances was the first step towards achieving financial freedom and living the life she always dreamed of.

Money is not just a tool for buying things; it is a concept that affects every aspect of our lives. As the famous investor Warren Buffett once said, "The most important thing to do if you find yourself in a hole is to stop digging." This quote emphasizes the importance of managing our money and not spending beyond our means. By understanding the true value of money and how it works, we can avoid getting into debt and build a solid financial foundation for ourselves.

To become financially literate, it is important to have a basic understanding of money, how it works, and how to manage it wisely. This can be achieved by reading books and articles on personal finance, attending financial workshops, or taking online courses. Developing good money habits such as creating a budget, saving regularly, and investing wisely can help us achieve our financial goals and build wealth over time.

In conclusion, understanding money is the first step towards managing our finances wisely and achieving financial success. Money is a complex concept, but with the right knowledge and tools, we can master its intricacies and use it to our advantage. By learning about personal finance and practicing good money habits, we can take control of our financial future and achieve our goals.

DIFFERENT TYPES OF MONEY

As Maya continued reading she learned about the different types of money in more detail.

She discovered that fiat money, which is the type of money used in most countries today, is backed by the government and has no intrinsic value. Its value is based on the trust people have in the government and the economy.

On the other hand, commodity money, such as gold or silver, has intrinsic value because of its usefulness in trade and commerce. Maya found it fascinating how people used to trade goods for precious metals like gold and silver, which later became standardized as

currency.

Maya also learned about digital money, which is becoming increasingly popular with the rise of technology. She discovered that digital money, such as cryptocurrency, operates on a decentralized system and offers a secure and transparent way to exchange value without the need for intermediaries like banks.

As Maya read more about the different types of money, she realized that each had its advantages and disadvantages. She learned that understanding the type of money she was using was crucial to making informed financial decisions.

Maya was particularly interested in digital money and decided to explore it further. She downloaded a cryptocurrency wallet and started investing in different cryptocurrencies. She found the decentralized system and the transparency of the transactions fascinating.

Maya also discovered the importance of diversifying her investments to manage risks. She invested in various types of assets, including stocks, bonds, and cryptocurrencies, to ensure her portfolio was well-balanced.

Through her exploration of the different types of money, Maya realized that being knowledgeable about finance was empowering. She felt more in control of her finances and confident in her ability to make informed financial decisions. Maya was grateful for the knowledge she had gained and was excited to continue her financial journey.

THE HISTORY OF MONEY

Money has a fascinating and often quirky history that can make it fun to learn about.

For example, did you know that the first recorded use of money was in ancient Mesopotamia around 3000 BC? The Mesopotamians used barley as a form of currency and even had a standardized unit of measurement for it. Imagine going to the store and buying a loaf of bread with a bag of barley!

Or how about this - the word "salary" actually comes from the Latin word "salarium," which referred to the salt rations that Roman soldiers were paid with. Salt was a valuable commodity in ancient times, and it was used as a form of currency in some parts of the world.

Another interesting tidbit is that cowrie shells were used as currency in many parts of the world, including Africa, Asia, and the Pacific Islands. These small shells were prized for their beauty and durability and were even used to make jewelry.

And let's not forget about the wild and wacky world of cryptocurrency! Did you know that the first cryptocurrency, Bitcoin, was created in 2009 by an unknown person using the pseudonym Satoshi Nakamoto? It's true! And today, there are thousands of different cryptocurrencies, each with its unique features and quirks.

Learning about the history of money can be both fascinating and entertaining, and it's an excellent way to understand how money has evolved over time.

RECOMMENDATIONS

Here are some learning sources that can help you understand money, its history, and how it works:

1. "The Ascent of Money: A Financial History of the World" by Niall Ferguson - This book provides a comprehensive history of money, from the bartering system to modern financial systems.
2. "The History of Money" by Jack Weatherford - This book traces the evolution of money from ancient civilizations to modern times.
3. "Money, Banking and Financial Markets" by Stephen Cecchetti and Kermit Schoenholtz - This textbook provides a comprehensive overview of the financial system and how it works.
4. "The Federal Reserve and the Financial Crisis" by Ben S. Bernanke - This book provides an insider's view of the financial crisis of 2008 and how the Federal Reserve responded.
5. "The Bitcoin Standard: The Decentralized Alternative to Central Banking" by Saifedean Ammous - This book provides an in-depth analysis of the history and principles of Bitcoin and the potential impact of decentralized currencies on the financial system.

CHAPTER 2: BUDGETING

John was a hardworking man, a skilled carpenter who took pride in his work. He had a wife and two children, and he did everything he could to provide for his family. But despite his best efforts, he found himself struggling to make ends meet.

One day, John came home from work to find that his wife was upset. She had received a notice from their landlord that their rent was going up, and they could no longer afford to live in their apartment. John felt the weight of the world on his shoulders. He had been working so hard, but it seemed like no matter how much he earned, it was never enough.

He tried to work harder and take on more jobs, but it only seemed to make things worse. The more he worked, the more he spent, and the more he struggled to keep up with his bills. John knew he needed to do something to get his finances in order, but he didn't know where to start.

That's when John decided to sit down and take a hard look at his finances. He started by tracking all of his expenses and creating a budget to see where his money was going. He was surprised to see that he was spending more than he realized on things like eating out and entertainment.

With his budget in place, John was able to see where he could make cuts and prioritize his spending. He started cooking more meals at home and bringing his lunch to work instead of eating out. He also found ways to entertain his family without spending a lot of money, like having picnics in the park or playing board games at home.

Slowly but surely, John's financial situation began to improve. He was able to pay off some of his debts and save up for emergencies. He even started putting money aside for his children's education.

John realized that budgeting wasn't just about cutting back on expenses, but about prioritizing what was important to him and his family. He felt a sense of empowerment and control over his finances that he had never felt before.

In the end, John was able to find a more affordable apartment for his family and was able to provide for them without feeling overwhelmed by debt and financial stress. He knew that budgeting was a lifelong habit that he would need to maintain, but he also knew that it was the key to his financial success.

HOW TO CREATE A BUDGET

Creating a budget is a crucial step in managing your finances and achieving your financial goals. Here are some tips and advice on how to create a budget:

1. Determine Your Income: The first step is to calculate your total income for a month. This includes your salary, any side hustles or freelance work, and any other sources of income.
2. List Your Expenses: Make a list of all your monthly expenses, including fixed expenses like rent or mortgage payments, utilities, insurance premiums, and other regular payments. Then, list out variable expenses like groceries, dining out, entertainment, and any other expenses that vary from month to month.
3. Categorize Your Expenses: Categorize your expenses into needs and wants. Needs are essential expenses that you cannot live without, like food, shelter, and healthcare. Wants are non-essential expenses like dining out, entertainment, and shopping.
4. Set Financial Goals: Determine your financial goals and prioritize them. Whether it's paying off debt, saving for a down payment on a house, or setting up an emergency fund, having clear financial goals can help you stay focused and motivated.
5. Allocate Your Income: Allocate your income based on your expenses and financial goals. Make sure to prioritize your needs and financial goals first, and then allocate the remaining funds to your wants.
6. Monitor and Adjust: Once you have created your budget, it is essential to monitor your spending to ensure that you are sticking to your budget. You may need to adjust your budget based on changes in income, expenses, or financial goals.

Some tricks and advice for creating a budget:

- Use budgeting tools like apps or software to help you track your expenses and monitor your budget.

- Set realistic financial goals and break them down into smaller, achievable goals to help you stay motivated.
- Cut back on unnecessary expenses and find ways to save money on essential expenses like groceries and utilities.
- Consider using cash instead of credit cards to help you stick to your budget and avoid overspending.
- Don't forget to include occasional expenses like car maintenance, holidays, or birthday gifts in your budget.

Creating a budget can take some time and effort, but it is a crucial step in achieving financial stability and achieving your financial goals. Remember to be flexible and adjust your budget as needed to help you stay on track.

TRACKING YOUR INCOME AND EXPENSES

Chapter 2 of "Smart Money" focuses on budgeting, which involves tracking your income and expenses to help you make informed financial decisions. John, likely started by identifying all of his sources of income and categorizing them, such as by paycheck, side gig, or investment income.

Some examples of types of income John is earning include:

1. Wages or salary: John has a regular job that pays him a set amount of money each month or week.
2. Self-employment income: John has a side business or freelance work that generates income on a project-by-project basis.
3. Investment income: John has investments that generate income, such as dividends from stocks or interest from

bonds.

4. Rental income: John owns rental property and earns income from collecting rent payments.

5. Retirement income: John is receiving income from a retirement account, such as a 401(k) or IRA.

Then John identified his expenses by keeping a log of all the money he spent over a period of time, such as a week or a month. This helped him see where his money was going and what expenses were essential and which were not.

After keeping the log, John categorized his expenses into different points such as:

1. Housing expenses: This includes rent/mortgage payments, utilities, and maintenance costs.

2. Transportation expenses: This includes gas, car maintenance, and public transportation costs.

3. Food and groceries expenses: This includes all expenses related to food and groceries, such as dining out, groceries, and snacks.

4. Entertainment expenses: This includes all expenses related to entertainment, such as movies, concerts, and hobbies.

5. Debt and loan payments: This includes all debt and loan payments, such as credit card bills, student loans, and car payments.

6. Miscellaneous expenses: This includes all other expenses, such as clothing, personal care items, and gifts.

By categorizing his expenses into these points, John was able to see where he was spending the most money and where he could potentially cut back on expenses. This helped him create a budget and better manage his finances.

Once John has identified all of his sources of income and expenses, John gained a clearer understanding of where his money is going and make adjustments as needed to achieve his financial goals.

SETTING FINANCIAL GOALS

Setting financial goals is crucial for achieving financial success. Financial goals help us create a roadmap for our financial journey, allowing us to prioritize our spending, save for the future, and invest in our long-term goals. By setting clear and achievable financial goals, we can stay focused and motivated, making it easier to resist temptations to overspend or give in to impulse purchases. Financial goals also help us measure our progress and make adjustments along the way, ensuring we stay on track towards our desired financial outcomes. Overall, setting financial goals is an important step towards financial well-being and a more secure future.

1. Pay off debt: John has a credit card debt, a car loan, or other outstanding loans that he wanted to pay off as quickly as possible to avoid accruing interest and fees.
2. Build an emergency fund: John has set a goal to save up three to six months' worth of expenses in an emergency fund to prepare for unexpected expenses or a job loss.
3. Save for children's education: John has set a goal to start saving for his children's college education to ensure they have the funds they need to pursue higher education.

4. Save for retirement: He has set a goal to start saving for his retirement to ensure he has enough money to live comfortably in his golden years.

5. Reduce expenses: He also has set a goal to find ways to cut back on his expenses, such as by negotiating bills or finding ways to reduce his grocery bill, in order to free up more money for savings or debt repayment.

By setting specific financial goals, John was able to focus his efforts and create a budget that helped him achieve those goals. This can be a helpful strategy for anyone looking to take control of their finances and improve their financial situation.

CHAPTER 3: SAVINGS

Alex was thrilled to land his first job after graduating from college. He had big plans for his future, and he was eager to start earning his own income. However, things didn't go exactly as he had planned. Alex soon found himself struggling to make ends meet, as he was living paycheck to paycheck and barely had any savings.

The problem was that Alex had never learned how to manage his finances properly. He had always relied on his parents to take care of his expenses, and he never realized how quickly money could disappear. With his new job, Alex was finally earning a decent salary, but he had no idea how to make the most of it.

One day, Alex stumbled upon an article about the importance of saving money. He realized that he needed to change his spending habits and start setting aside some of his income for a rainy day. He began by creating a budget and identifying his expenses. He cut back on unnecessary expenses, such as eating out and buying expensive gadgets, and started putting money into a savings account.

At first, it was difficult for Alex to adjust to his new lifestyle. He had to say no to his friends' invitations to go out and spend money, and he had to learn to live within his means. However, as he began to see his savings grow, he felt a sense of pride and accomplishment. He realized that he was in control of his financial future and that he could achieve his goals if he managed his money wisely.

Through discipline and dedication, Alex was able to overcome his financial struggles and build a solid foundation for his future. He learned that saving money is not just about having extra cash in the bank; it's about having the peace of mind that comes with knowing you can handle unexpected expenses and achieve your financial goals.

IMPORTANCE OF SAVING MONEY

Saving money is an essential part of financial planning. It can be difficult to do, especially when you have a lot of bills to pay, but it's important to make it a priority. Alex learned this the hard way.

At the beginning of the story, Alex was living paycheck to paycheck. He spent money on things he didn't need and didn't save any for emergencies or future goals. This left him in a precarious financial situation, as he had no safety net to fall back on when unexpected expenses arose.

One day, Alex's car broke down and he had to pay for an expensive repair. Because he hadn't saved any money, he had to put the cost on his credit card, which only added to his debt. This was a wake-up call for Alex, and he realized that he needed to start saving money if he wanted to avoid this kind of situation in the future.

Saving money is important because it allows you to have a safety net for emergencies, like car repairs or unexpected medical bills. It also enables you to work towards your financial goals, like buying a home, starting a business, or saving for retirement. By setting aside a portion of your income each month, you can gradually build up a savings account that will provide you with financial security and peace of mind.

Alex learned the importance of saving money the hard way, but he was able to turn his financial situation around by making saving a priority. He started by setting a savings goal and creating a budget that allowed him to set aside a certain amount of money each month. He also looked for ways to cut back on his expenses, like eating out less and canceling subscriptions he didn't use.

Over time, Alex's savings account grew, and he was able to pay off his credit card debt and start saving for a down payment on a house. He felt more secure in his financial situation and had a sense of pride knowing that he was in control of his money.

In conclusion, saving money is an essential part of financial planning. It allows you to have a safety net for emergencies and work towards your financial goals. Alex learned this the hard way, but he was able to turn his financial situation around by making saving a priority. By setting a savings goal, creating a budget, and looking for ways to cut back on expenses, anyone can start building their savings account and working towards a brighter financial future.

STRATEGIES FOR BUILDING YOUR SAVING

Alex used various strategies to build his savings, such as:

1. Creating a budget: Alex tracked his income and expenses and created a budget to help him identify areas where he could cut back on expenses and save more money.
2. Setting financial goals: Alex set specific financial goals, such as saving for a down payment on a house, and worked towards achieving them.
3. Automating savings: Alex set up automatic transfers from his checking account to his savings account, so that he was consistently saving a portion of his income without having to think about it.
4. Cutting back on expenses: Alex made a conscious effort to cut back on unnecessary expenses, such as eating out and buying expensive clothes.
5. Increasing his income: Alex also looked for ways to increase

his income, such as taking on a part-time job or starting a side hustle.

By implementing these strategies, Alex was able to build his savings and achieve his financial goals. You too can use these strategies to build your savings and achieve financial stability.

CHAPTER 4: DEBIT AND CREDIT

We meet Ava, a recent divorcee who is struggling with her finances. Ava had always been cautious with her money, but one day she found herself facing an unexpected medical bill that she couldn't afford to pay in full. She decided to put the bill on her credit card, thinking she could pay it off over time.

At first, Ava was able to make the minimum payments on her credit card each month, but eventually the interest started to add up and she found herself in a cycle of debt. She knew she needed to do something to break free from this cycle and get her finances back on track.

Understanding Debt and Credit

Ava realized that she needed to learn more about how debt and credit work in order to manage her finances wisely. She started by learning the difference between good debt and bad debt. Good debt is debt that helps you build wealth, such as a mortgage or student loans, while bad debt is debt that doesn't provide any long-term benefits, such as credit card debt.

Managing and Paying Off Debt

Ava then learned some strategies for managing and paying off debt. She focused on paying off her credit card debt first, since it had the highest interest rate. She also looked into options for consolidating her debt, such as taking out a personal loan with a lower interest rate or transferring her credit card balances to a card with a 0% introductory rate.

Building and Maintaining Good Credit

Finally, Ava learned about the importance of building and maintaining good credit. She learned that having good credit can help her get approved for loans and credit cards with favorable terms, while bad credit can make it difficult to get approved or result in higher interest rates.

Ava made a plan to pay off her debt and improve her credit score. She set a budget to pay down her debt as quickly as possible and made sure to make all of her payments on time. She also checked her credit report regularly to ensure there were no errors or fraudulent activity.

Conclusion

Through her journey of learning about debt and credit, Ava was able to break free from her cycle of debt and take control of her finances. She learned the importance of managing debt wisely and building good credit, which will serve her well in the future.

UNDERSTANDING DEBIT AND CREDIT

Debit and credit are two fundamental terms in the world of finance. Both terms are used to indicate whether money is being added to an account (credit) or subtracted from an account (debit). The concepts of debit and credit have been around for centuries and have evolved over time to meet the changing needs of the economy.

The origins of debit and credit can be traced back to the Italian Renaissance. Italian merchants used a double-entry accounting system to keep track of their finances. The system was based on the principles of debits and credits, which allowed merchants to record their financial transactions accurately and efficiently.

Today, the terms debit and credit are used in a variety of financial contexts. In banking, debit refers to the removal of funds from an account, while credit refers to the addition of funds to an account. Credit cards allow users to make purchases on credit, which they must later repay with interest. Debit cards, on the other hand, allow users to make purchases using funds from their bank account.

There are also different types of debit and credit accounts. Checking accounts are typically debit accounts, as funds are removed from the account when purchases are made. Savings accounts, on the other hand, are typically credit accounts, as interest is added to the account over time.

It is important to use debit and credit wisely to avoid financial difficulties. Using a credit card irresponsibly can lead to debt and financial ruin. However, using a credit card responsibly can help build a good credit score, which can be beneficial for future loans and financial opportunities.

When using debit and credit, it is important to keep track of your transactions and account balances. Monitoring your spending habits and creating a budget can help you avoid overspending and ensure that you have enough funds to cover your expenses.

In conclusion, debit and credit are essential concepts in the world of finance. Understanding how they work and how to use them wisely is important for managing your finances effectively. Whether you are using a credit card, debit card, or any other financial account, it is important to stay informed and make responsible financial decisions.

THE DANGERS OF DEBT

Debt is like quicksand – it's easy to get in, but hard to get out of. Debt refers to the money borrowed by an individual, company, or government that needs to be repaid with interest over time. While debt can be a useful tool to finance purchases or investments, it can also be dangerous and can also be a slippery slope to financial trouble if you're not careful.

One of the dangers of debt is that it can lead to financial stress and anxiety. Debt can pile up quickly and become overwhelming, leaving individuals feeling trapped and hopeless. It can also lead to strained relationships and impact mental health.

Another danger of debt is that it can become a cycle that is difficult to break. High-interest rates and fees can make it difficult to pay off debts, leading to more borrowing to make ends meet. This cycle can continue indefinitely, leading to a lifetime of financial hardship.

A short story illustrating the dangers of debt is that of Emily, a young woman who fell into credit card debt after using them to pay for everyday expenses like groceries and bills. At first, she was able to make the minimum payments, but as the balance grew, she found herself struggling to keep up. The high-interest rates made it difficult to make any real progress on paying down the debt, and she found herself living paycheck to paycheck. The stress of the debt began to impact her mental health and relationships, and she realized that she needed to take action to get out of the cycle of debt.

Famous people have also spoken about the dangers of debt. Dave Ramsey, a personal finance expert, once said, "Debt is not a tool. It is a method to make banks wealthy, not you." This quote emphasizes the idea that debt can be dangerous if not managed properly, and that it is important to take control of your finances and avoid unnecessary debt.

In conclusion, while debt can be useful in certain circumstances, it is important to understand the dangers it can pose to our financial and mental well-being. It is essential to manage debt responsibly, make a plan to pay it off, and avoid taking on unnecessary debt.

HOW TO MANAGE AND PAY OFF YOUR DEBT

Once Ava realized the dangers of debt, she knew she had to take action to manage and pay off her existing debts. Here are some tips and tricks she used that may be helpful to others in a similar situation:

1. Create a budget: This is a critical step in managing debt. By creating a budget, you can see exactly how much money you have coming in and going out each month. This will allow you to identify areas where you can cut back on spending and allocate more money towards paying off your debts.
2. Prioritize your debts: Not all debts are created equal. Some may have higher interest rates or more severe consequences if they go unpaid. Prioritize your debts by tackling the ones with the highest interest rates or those that are most overdue first.
3. Negotiate with creditors: Don't be afraid to reach out to your creditors to negotiate repayment terms or interest rates. Many creditors are willing to work with you to come up with a repayment plan that is feasible for your situation.
4. Consider debt consolidation: If you have multiple debts with high interest rates, consolidating them into one loan with a lower interest rate may be a good option. This can make it easier to manage your debt and reduce your overall interest payments.

5. Focus on the long-term: Paying off debt can be a long and difficult process, but it's important to stay focused on the end goal. Visualize the relief and financial freedom you will experience once your debts are paid off, and use that as motivation to stay on track.

Ava used these tips and tricks to successfully manage and pay off her debts. While it wasn't easy, she remained committed to her goal and eventually achieved financial freedom.

BUILDING AND MAINTAINING GOOD CREDIT

After successfully paying off her debts, Ava became interested in building and maintaining good credit. She knew that a good credit score would enable her to access credit in the future at lower interest rates, making it easier for her to achieve her financial goals.

Ava started by checking her credit report to ensure that all information was accurate and up-to-date. She learned that she could get a free credit report from each of the three major credit reporting agencies once a year. She made sure to keep an eye on her credit report regularly, so that she could quickly detect any errors or fraudulent activity.

Ava also learned that one of the best ways to build credit was to make timely payments on her bills and debts. She set up automatic payments for her bills and made sure to pay her credit card balances in full each month. This helped her to avoid late fees and high interest charges, while also demonstrating to lenders that she was responsible with credit.

Another way that Ava built her credit was by using credit responsibly.

She only applied for credit when she needed it and made sure to only use a small portion of her available credit. This helped to keep her credit utilization low, which is an important factor in determining credit scores.

By following these tips and tricks, Ava was able to maintain a good credit score and access credit at lower interest rates when she needed it. She felt more financially secure knowing that she had built a strong financial foundation for herself.

CHAPTER 5: INVESTING

Carlos is a retiree who wants to grow his wealth but is hesitant to start investing, but he's also worried about his financial future. He wants to make sure he's saving and investing his money wisely so that allows him to achieve his financial goals and live comfortably in retirement.

Carlos decides to learn about investing, and he begins by reading books and articles on the subject. He learns about the different types of investments, including stocks, bonds, mutual funds, and real estate. He also learns about the risks and rewards of each type of investment.

As he continues his research, Carlos realizes that he needs to develop a long-term investment strategy that will help him achieve his goals. He decides to start by setting some financial goals, just as John did when he created his budget. So, what exactly is investing?

Investing is the act of committing money or capital to an endeavor with the expectation of obtaining additional income or profit. It is essentially putting money to work in order to earn a return. Investing can take many forms, such as stocks, bonds, real estate, mutual funds, and exchange-traded funds (ETFs), among others.

The primary goal of investing is to grow one's wealth over time. By investing wisely, individuals can generate passive income, protect themselves against inflation, and build long-term financial security. Investing can also provide a means to achieve financial goals, such as buying a home or saving for retirement.

Investing has a long and storied history. Ancient civilizations, such as the Egyptians and Greeks, used investing to finance large construction projects and other endeavors. In the modern era, investing has become more accessible to individuals through the growth of financial markets and the rise of online trading platforms.

There are many different types of investments, each with its own level of risk and potential reward. Stocks, for example, offer the potential for high returns but also come with a greater risk of loss. Bonds, on the other hand, are generally considered safer but offer lower returns. Real estate investing can offer significant long-term returns, but also requires a significant upfront investment.

Investing can be a complex and intimidating subject for many individuals, but it is an important part of achieving financial success. By understanding the basics of investing and working with a trusted financial advisor, individuals can make informed decisions and build a strong investment portfolio.

Famous investors, such as Warren Buffett and Peter Lynch, have espoused the importance of investing throughout their careers. Buffett, often referred to as the "Oracle of Omaha," has famously advised investors to "be fearful when others are greedy and greedy when others are fearful." Lynch, who achieved significant success as a mutual fund manager, has emphasized the importance of conducting thorough research and investing in companies with strong fundamentals.

In summary, investing is a key tool for building long-term financial security and achieving financial goals. By understanding the history, types, and potential risks and rewards of investing, individuals can make informed decisions and grow their wealth over time.

Back to the story of Carlos, Once he has his goals in place, Carlos begins to research specific investments that can help him achieve them. He decides to start by investing in a diversified portfolio of mutual funds and in real estate. He also sets up a retirement account and begins contributing to it regularly

Over time, Carlos's investments begin to grow, and he feels more secure about his financial future. He's also happy to see that his credit score has improved, thanks to his responsible use of credit and his timely payments on his debts.

Carlos's success with investing has given him the confidence to take on more financial responsibilities, and he's excited to see where his investments will take him in the future.

WHY INVESTING IS IMPORTANT

Investing is important because it allows you to grow your money over time, which can help you achieve your financial goals. Instead of simply saving money in a bank account, where it may earn very little interest, investing allows you to put your money to work in the market, potentially earning higher returns.

There are a few reasons why investing is important:

1. Beat inflation: Inflation is the gradual increase in the cost of goods and services over time. If your money is not growing at least as fast as inflation, you're effectively losing money. Investing can help you beat inflation and maintain the purchasing power of your money.
2. Compound interest: Investing allows you to take advantage of compound interest, which means that your money earns

interest on the interest it has already earned. Over time, this can lead to significant growth in your investments.

3. Achieve long-term financial goals: Investing can help you achieve long-term financial goals, such as retirement or buying a home. By starting early and investing consistently over time, you can potentially build a significant nest egg.

A story of a person who found out the importance of investing after getting into trouble is Tom. Tom was a hardworking man who had always provided for his family. He had a good job, a comfortable house, and enough money to pay his bills. However, when his daughter Sarah was ready to go to college, Tom realized that he had not saved enough money to pay for her education.

Tom had always thought that he could save enough money by just working hard and being frugal. He had never given much importance to investing his money. But now, he was faced with the harsh reality that he had not prepared enough for his daughter's education.

Tom was worried and stressed about how he would pay for Sarah's college tuition. He started exploring his options and realized that he could have avoided this situation if he had invested his money wisely. He regretted not paying attention to the importance of investing earlier.

Tom started educating himself about investing and started investing a portion of his income regularly and was amazed at how his money started to grow. He realized that investing was not just about making money but also about achieving his financial goals.

Tom's experience taught him a valuable lesson about the importance of investing. He realized that by investing his money wisely, he could achieve his financial goals and secure his family's future.

Investing is a crucial part of personal finance, as it provides an opportunity to grow wealth over time and achieve financial goals. As billionaire investor Warren Buffett once said, "If you don't find a way to make money while you sleep, you will work until you die." Investing helps individuals to generate passive income and build a secure financial future for themselves and their loved ones.

THE DIFFERENT TYPES OF INVESTMENTS

There are several different types of investing that people can choose from based on their financial goals, risk tolerance, and investment horizon. Here are some of the most common types of investing:

1. Stocks: Stocks represent ownership in a company and can be bought and sold on stock exchanges. They are a popular type of investment for those seeking long-term growth.
2. Bonds: Bonds are debt instruments issued by companies or governments. Investors lend money to the issuer and receive interest payments over time, with the principal returned at maturity. Bonds are typically less risky than stocks but offer lower returns.
3. Mutual funds: Mutual funds are professionally managed portfolios of stocks, bonds, and other securities. They offer investors a diversified way to invest in a variety of assets with one investment.
4. Exchange-Traded Funds (ETFs): ETFs are similar to mutual funds, but they trade on stock exchanges like individual stocks. They also offer investors a diversified way to invest in a variety of assets.
5. Real Estate: Real estate can be a good investment for those seeking income or long-term appreciation. Investors can buy

rental properties or participate in real estate investment trusts (REITs).

6. Alternative investments: Alternative investments include commodities, hedge funds, private equity, and other non-traditional investments. These are often only available to accredited investors and can be risky.

It's important to note that each type of investment carries its own risks and rewards, and investors should carefully consider their options before making any investment decisions.

RISKS AND REWARD OF INVESTING

Investing involves taking a risk with your money in the hopes of gaining a reward. The risk and reward of investing can vary depending on the type of investment you choose.

The main risks of investing include the possibility of losing money, not earning the expected returns, and the uncertainty of the future. Some investments, such as stocks and cryptocurrencies, can be particularly volatile and their value can fluctuate rapidly. It's important to remember that all investments come with a certain level of risk.

On the other hand, the rewards of investing can be substantial. The potential to earn a high return on your investment is one of the main reasons why people invest. Additionally, investing can help you beat inflation, grow your wealth over time, and achieve financial goals such as retirement.

It's important to note that the level of risk and reward of investing is directly related. Generally, investments with higher risks offer higher potential rewards. Before investing, it's important to carefully consider your risk tolerance and investment goals to determine the appropriate level of risk for your situation. Additionally, diversifying your investments can help mitigate risk and increase potential rewards.

HOW TO START INVESTING

Carlos knew that investing was important to grow his wealth over time, but he wasn't sure where to start. After doing some research, he learned about different investment options, such as stocks, bonds, and mutual funds, real-estate and some alternative assets.

To start investing, Carlos opened a brokerage account with a reputable online broker. He made sure to compare the fees and features of different brokers to find one that suited his needs.

Carlos then decided to invest in a diversified portfolio of low-cost index funds, which gave him exposure to a broad range of stocks and bonds. He set up automatic contributions to his investment account each month, which allowed him to invest regularly without having to think about it.

Carlos also continued to educate himself about investing by reading books and articles, watching videos, and following financial experts on social media. He learned how to rebalance his portfolio periodically to maintain his desired asset allocation and minimize risk.

Through consistent investing and a long-term perspective, Carlos was able to grow his wealth and achieve his financial goals.

Carlos was always interested in investing, but he wasn't quite sure where to start. He had read about stocks and bonds, but he was looking for something more tangible, something he could see and touch. That's when he started to consider investing in real estate.

He began by doing some research, reading books and articles about the real estate market and attending seminars and workshops. He learned about different types of real estate investments, including residential properties, commercial properties, and raw land. He also learned about the risks and rewards of investing in real estate.

Carlos started small by investing in a rental property. He purchased a small apartment building and began renting out the units. The rental income provided a steady stream of passive income, which he could reinvest in other real estate properties.

As Carlos gained more experience and confidence, he began exploring alternative investments. He learned about peer-to-peer lending, crowdfunding, and investing in startups. He invested in a few startups that he believed had the potential for high returns.

Investing in alternative assets helped Carlos diversify his investment portfolio and reduce his overall risk. He also found that he enjoyed the challenge of researching and evaluating new investment opportunities.

Overall, Carlos found that investing in Stock, bonds, real estate and alternative assets had been a smart decision. His investments had provided him with a solid financial foundation and had given him the freedom to pursue his passions and dreams.

RECOMMENDATIONS

Here are some recommended books, articles, and resources on the topics of stocks, bonds, mutual funds, ETFs, real estate, and alternative investments:

1. "The Intelligent Investor" by Benjamin Graham
2. "A Random Walk Down Wall Street" by Burton Malkiel
3. "The Bogleheads' Guide to Investing" by Taylor Larimore, Mel Lindauer, and Michael LeBoeuf
4. "The Little Book of Common Sense Investing" by John C. Bogle
5. "The Essays of Warren Buffett: Lessons for Corporate America" by Warren E. Buffett and Lawrence A. Cunningham
6. "The Millionaire Real Estate Investor" by Gary Keller, Dave Jenks, and Jay Papasan
7. "The Book on Rental Property Investing" by Brandon Turner
8. "Rich Dad Poor Dad" by Robert T. Kiyosaki
9. "Investing in Your 20s and 30s For Dummies" by Eric Tyson
10. "Investopedia" website for a comprehensive guide on financial topics.

These resources can provide valuable insights and information for anyone looking to invest in various areas of the market.

CHAPTER 6: BUILDING WEALTH

Sarah is a successful business owner and she wants to be financially independent. She learns strategies for building wealth, such as creating passive income streams and investing in real estate. With a solid plan in place, Sarah is able to achieve her goal of financial independence and live the life she always dreamed of

Sarah starts by creating a budget and setting financial goals for herself. She wants to save up enough money to buy a house, travel the world, and eventually retire comfortably. She also wants to start investing her money to grow her wealth.

To create passive income streams, Sarah starts a side hustle selling handmade crafts online. She also invests in dividend-paying stocks and real estate investment trusts (REITs) that provide a steady stream of passive income.

To build a diversified investment portfolio, Sarah invests in a mix of stocks, bonds, mutual funds, and ETFs. She researches different investment options and consults with a financial advisor to ensure she is making smart investment decisions.

Sarah also works hard to achieve financial independence by living below her means, avoiding debt, and constantly growing her wealth. She knows that achieving financial independence will give her the freedom to live life on her own terms and pursue her passions without financial stress.

As Sarah continues to build her wealth, she learns that it's not just about making more money, but also about being smart with the money you have. She feels empowered knowing that she has the knowledge and tools to manage her finances wisely and achieve her financial goals.

CREATING PASSIVE INCOME STREAMS

Passive income streams are an important aspect of building wealth, as they generate regular income without requiring active effort. Sarah learned about various strategies to create passive income streams, including:

1. Rental properties: Sarah invested in rental properties and became a landlord, earning rental income each month.
2. Dividend stocks: She invested in stocks that paid regular dividends, which added to her passive income stream.
3. Peer-to-peer lending: Sarah invested in peer-to-peer lending platforms, where she lent money to individuals and received regular interest payments.
4. Royalties: Sarah created intellectual property such as books, music, or software and received royalties each time her work was sold or used.
5. Creating an online business: She started an online business that generated passive income through advertising revenue, affiliate marketing, or selling digital products.

By diversifying her passive income streams, Sarah was able to create a steady stream of income that continued to grow over time, helping her achieve financial independence.

RECOMMENDATIONS

Sure, here are some recommendations for websites and books on creating passive income streams:

Websites:

1. Smart Passive Income - https://www.smartpassiveincome.com/
2. Side Hustle Nation - https://www.sidehustlenation.com/
3. The College Investor - https://thecollegeinvestor.com/

Books:

1. "The 4-Hour Work Week" by Timothy Ferriss
2. "Rich Dad Poor Dad" by Robert Kiyosaki
3. "The Power of Passive Income" by Nightingale-Conant Corporation
4. "Passive Income, Aggressive Retirement" by Rachel Richards
5. "The Ultimate Guide to Passive Income" by Derek Doepker.

BUILDING A DIVERSIFIED INVESTMENT PORTFOLIO

Building a diversified investment portfolio means investing in a variety of assets across different asset classes, sectors, and geographical regions to spread out the risk and maximize returns. A diversified portfolio typically includes a mix of stocks, bonds, cash, and alternative investments.

Here are some tips for building a diversified investment portfolio:

1. Determine your risk tolerance: Before you start investing, it's

important to understand your risk tolerance. This will help you choose the right mix of assets for your portfolio.

2. Choose a mix of asset classes: A well-diversified portfolio includes a mix of asset classes such as stocks, bonds, cash, and alternative investments. Each asset class has its own risk and return characteristics, so by investing in a mix of assets, you can spread out the risk and maximize returns.

3. Choose a mix of sectors: Within each asset class, there are different sectors such as technology, healthcare, energy, and financials. By investing in a mix of sectors, you can reduce the impact of any one sector's performance on your portfolio.

4. Invest across different geographical regions: Investing in different regions can help you diversify your portfolio and reduce the impact of any one country's economic performance on your portfolio.

5. Rebalance regularly: It's important to review your portfolio periodically and rebalance it to ensure that it remains diversified. As some investments perform better than others, your portfolio's asset allocation may become skewed. Rebalancing involves selling some of the outperforming assets and reinvesting the proceeds in underperforming assets to maintain your desired asset allocation.

Some resources for building a diversified investment portfolio include:

1. Bogleheads Guide to Investing by Taylor Larimore: This book provides a comprehensive guide to investing in a simple and straightforward manner, with an emphasis on building a diversified investment portfolio.

2. Morningstar: This website provides independent investment research and analysis, including tools to help you build and monitor a diversified investment portfolio.

3. Vanguard: This investment company offers a range of low-

cost index funds and ETFs that are designed to help investors build a diversified portfolio.

4. Charles Schwab: This investment company offers a range of investment products and services, including tools and resources to help investors build a diversified portfolio.

There are many websites that can help you build a diversified investment portfolio. Some popular ones include:

1. Betterment - an automated investing service that builds and manages your portfolio based on your goals and risk tolerance.
2. Wealthfront - a robo-advisor that creates a personalized investment plan and manages your portfolio for you.
3. Vanguard - a well-known investment management company that offers a variety of low-cost index funds and ETFs.
4. Fidelity - another popular investment management company that provides a range of investment options including stocks, mutual funds, and ETFs.
5. Morningstar - a financial research firm that provides analysis and ratings of different investment products.

It's important to do your own research and due diligence when selecting an investment platform, taking into consideration factors such as fees, investment options, and customer support.

ACHIEVING FINANCIAL INDEPENDENCE

Certainly! Achieving financial independence means having enough passive income to cover all of your expenses, so you no longer have to work for a paycheck. This can be achieved through a combination of smart budgeting, careful investing, and building multiple streams of passive income.

Sarah achieved financial independence by following these steps:

1. Creating a budget and living below her means: Sarah tracked her expenses and made sure that her spending was always less than her income. By keeping her expenses low, she was able to save more money to invest.
2. Investing in a diversified portfolio: Sarah invested in a mix of stocks, bonds, mutual funds, ETFs, and real estate to create a diversified portfolio that would generate steady returns over time.
3. Building passive income streams: Sarah also built several passive income streams, including rental properties, dividend-paying stocks, and a small business. By creating multiple streams of income, she reduced her reliance on any one source of income.
4. Continuously learning and growing her wealth: Sarah remained committed to learning about personal finance and investing throughout her journey. She regularly read books and articles, attended seminars and webinars, and sought out advice from financial experts.

By following these steps, Sarah was able to achieve financial independence and live a life free from financial worry that she dreamed of.

CHAPTER 7: MANAGING YOUR MONEY MINDSET

Congratulations! You have learned a lot about managing your money, building wealth, and achieving financial independence. But there is one more thing that you need to master - your money mindset.

Your money mindset is your beliefs and attitudes about money. It affects the way you earn, spend, save, and invest your money. If you have a negative money mindset, it can hold you back from reaching your financial goals. But if you have a positive money mindset, it can help you overcome obstacles and achieve financial success.

By cultivating a positive money mindset, you can overcome limiting beliefs and achieve financial success. Remember, your mindset is the most important factor in your financial journey. So, start working on it today and see the difference it makes in your life!

UNDERSTANDING YOUR RELATIONSHIP WITH MONEY

Understanding your relationship with money is one of the key factors in managing your finances wisely. Money is not just a piece of paper or a number in your bank account; it represents your values, beliefs, and emotions. Your relationship with money shapes your financial habits and decisions.

The book "Smart Money: How to Manage Your Finance Wisely" is designed to help you develop a positive relationship with money by providing practical advice and strategies for managing your finances effectively. It is not just about saving or investing money, but also about understanding your own financial behavior and developing healthy habits that will lead to long-term financial success.

By reading this book, you will learn how to set financial goals, create a budget, track your expenses, pay off debt, invest wisely, build wealth, and develop a positive money mindset. You will also learn from the stories of Maya, John, Ava, Alex, Carlos, and Sarah, who have overcome financial challenges and achieved financial success through smart money management.

Ultimately, the goal of this book is to empower you to take control of your finances, make informed financial decisions, and build a strong financial foundation that will enable you to achieve your life goals and dreams. So, let's dive in and start managing our money wisely!

OVERCOMING COMMON MONEY MINDSET OBSTACLES

Money mindset obstacles can often hold us back from making smart financial decisions and achieving our financial goals. Some common obstacles include:

1. Scarcity mindset: This is the belief that there is a limited amount of money or resources available, which can lead to fear and anxiety around money. It can also make us hesitant to spend money, even when it is necessary.
2. Impulse buying: Impulse buying is the tendency to make unplanned purchases without considering the long-term consequences. This can lead to overspending and a lack of savings.
3. Fear of investing: Many people are intimidated by the idea of investing and may avoid it altogether. However, investing is an important part of building wealth and achieving financial

independence.

4. Lack of financial education: Without a basic understanding of personal finance, it can be difficult to make informed decisions about saving, investing, and managing money.

To overcome these obstacles, it's important to cultivate a positive money mindset and develop healthy financial habits. This includes setting financial goals, creating a budget, tracking expenses, and educating yourself about personal finance. By taking small steps towards financial literacy and making intentional choices about money, you can overcome these obstacles and build a secure financial future.

DEVELOPING A HEALTHY AND POSITIVE MONEY MINDSET

Certainly! Here are some elaborations and explanations of the tips to cultivate a positive money mindset:

1. Practice gratitude: Take time each day to reflect on what you have and be grateful for it. This can help shift your focus from what you don't have to what you do have, which can increase your sense of abundance and decrease feelings of lack.

2. Visualize success: Imagine yourself achieving your financial goals and living the life you want. This can help motivate you to take action and make choices that align with your vision.

3. Reframe negative thoughts: Challenge negative thoughts about money and replace them with more positive ones. For example, instead of thinking "I'll never be able to afford that," reframe it to "I'm working towards being able to afford that in the future."

4. Focus on abundance: Instead of dwelling on scarcity and what you don't have, focus on abundance and what you do have. This can help shift your mindset from one of lack to one of possibility and growth.

5. Practice self-care: Take care of yourself physically, mentally, and emotionally. When you feel good, you're more likely to make positive choices and feel more optimistic about your financial future.

6. Educate yourself: Learn about personal finance and investing so you can make informed decisions about your money. Knowledge can help empower you and give you more confidence in your financial decisions.

7. Surround yourself with positivity: Surround yourself with people who have a positive money mindset and who support your financial goals. Being around negativity and naysayers can be draining and discourage you from pursuing your dreams.

Overall, cultivating a positive money mindset involves shifting your focus from scarcity and lack to abundance and growth, challenging negative thoughts, and taking care of yourself both physically and mentally. With a positive mindset, you'll be better equipped to make informed financial decisions, take action towards your goals, and achieve financial success.

RECOMMENDATIONS

Certainly! Here are some reading materials on building a positive money mindset:

1. "The Psychology of Money" by Morgan Housel

2. "Think and Grow Rich" by Napoleon Hill
3. "The Richest Man in Babylon" by George S. Clason
4. "The Millionaire Mind" by Thomas J. Stanley
5. "The Power of Your Subconscious Mind" by Joseph Murphy
6. "Rich Dad Poor Dad" by Robert Kiyosaki
7. "You Are a Badass at Making Money" by Jen Sincero
8. "The Simple Path to Wealth" by JL Collins
9. "The Automatic Millionaire" by David Bach
10. "The Total Money Makeover" by Dave Ramsey

These books provide practical tips, inspiration, and guidance to help build a positive money mindset and achieve financial success.

CONCLUSION

Being smart with your money is not always easy, but it is essential for achieving your financial goals and living the life you want. By understanding the basics of money management, budgeting, saving, debt and credit, investing, and building wealth, you can develop the skills and mindset needed to achieve financial success. Remember to always be disciplined, patient, and persistent, and never stop learning and growing on your financial journey.

Maya, John, Ava, Alex, Carlos, and Sarah had all come a long way on their financial journeys. They had learned about money, budgeting, managing debt, investing, building wealth, and cultivating a positive money mindset. They had faced challenges and overcome obstacles, but they never gave up.

One day, they all met at a conference on personal finance. They were surprised to see each other and excited to catch up on their progress. Maya shared how she had become a successful entrepreneur and she learned that understanding money was the first step in managing her finances wisely and achieving financial freedom, John talked about how he had paid off his debts and saved enough for his children's education ,he realized the importance of budgeting and tracking his expenses to take control of his finances, Ava explained how she had managed to build a good credit score and invest in stocks, Alex discovered the importance of saving and investing for his future after facing financial troubles, Carlos talked about his diversified investment portfolio and importance of investing and Sarah explained how she had achieved financial independence by creating multiple streams of passive income.

As they talked, they realized something special. They had all come from different backgrounds, faced different challenges, and had different goals, but they had all learned the same fundamental principles of personal finance. They all shared a passion for learning, a willingness to take risks, and a desire to achieve financial freedom.

With that realization, they decided to create a new project, a book that would share their experiences and insights with others. They would call it "Smart Money" and it would be a guide for anyone who wanted to take control of their finances and achieve their dreams.

Together, they worked tirelessly on the book, sharing their stories, their tips, and their advice. They poured their hearts and souls into it, knowing that it would make a difference in the lives of others. And they were right.

Years later, as they sat together at another conference, they looked back on their journey with pride and satisfaction. They had not only achieved their own financial goals but had also helped countless others to do the same. And they knew that their legacy would live on, inspiring generations to come.

As they raised a toast to each other, they knew that they had truly become masters of their money and their lives. And they smiled, knowing that they had done something truly special together.

ALWAYS REMEMBER:

"Money is only a tool. It will take you wherever you wish, but it will not replace you as the driver." - Ayn Rand

AFTERWORD

Dear readers,

I hope that reading "Smart Money: How to Manage Your Finances Wisely" has been a valuable experience for you. Managing your finances can seem like a daunting task, but with the right knowledge and tools, it can be a rewarding journey towards financial freedom and security. Throughout this book, we have explored various topics related to personal finance, including budgeting, saving, investing, understanding debt and credit, and the importance of financial education. We have seen how individuals like Maya, John, Ava, Alex, Carlos, and Sarah have faced financial challenges and learned to overcome them through practical advice and sound financial principles. I hope that you have gained valuable insights into the world of finance and learned how to apply them to your own life. Remember, financial success is not just about making more money, but also about managing it wisely. I encourage you to take action and apply what you have learned in this book. Set financial goals, create a budget, start saving and investing, and seek out resources to continue your financial education. Thank for taking the time to read "Smart Money." I wish you all the best in your financial journey.

Sincerely,

Your Friend

[Avin Alexander Inkwell]

www.ingramcontent.com/pod-product-compliance
Lightning Source LLC
Chambersburg PA
CBHW070516220526
45467CB00002B/685